poo jokebook

Other bang on the door™© titles available:

For younger readers
Silly Billy
Drama Queen

For older readers
Friends
Friends Again

bang on the door™©

poo jokebook

An imprint of HarperCollins*Publishers*

First published in 2003 in Great Britain
by HarperCollins Publishers Ltd.

1 3 5 7 9 8 6 4 2

ISBN: 0-00-715214-0

Bang on the door character copyright:
© 2003 Bang on the Door all rights reserved.
⊕ bang on the door *ⓒ is a trademark
Exclusive right to license by Santoro

www.bangonthedoor.com

Text © 2003 HarperCollins Publishers Ltd

A CIP catalogue record for this title
is available from the British Library.

The HarperCollins website address is: www.**fire**and**water**.com

Printed and bound in Great Britain by Clays Ltd, St Ives plc.

wicked whiffs

What does the Queen
do if she breaks wind?
Issues a Royal Pardon!

Who was the smelliest Royal ever?
King Pong!

How do you make a toilet roll?

Throw it down a hill!

Where would a gnome go if he had a wind problem?

The elf centre!

haha**ha**

What do you call a woman with two toilets on her head?
Lulu!

What tree can't you climb?
A lavatory!

What do you call a man with a toilet on his head?
John!

What do you clean
your top teeth with?
A toothbrush
And?
Some toothpaste
What do you clean
your bottom with?
The same
Oh gross, I use toilet paper!

What's brown
and sticky?
A stick!

When can't a
steam engine
sit down?
When it has a
tender behind!

I'm going to have to let one rip,
do you mind?
Not if you don't mind if I throw up!

What vegetable can you
find in the toilet?
A leek!

What famous artist had toilets upstairs
and downstairs?
Toulouse Lautrec!

Why do traffic lights go red?
*Well you would go red if you had to stop
and go in the middle of the road!*

What's a sick joke?
*Something you
shouldn't bring up in
conversation!*

Why did Captain Kirk, Spock and Bones go to the ladies toilet?
To boldly go where no man had been before!

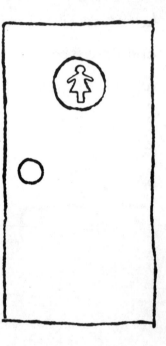

Did you hear the joke about the cesspit?
No? Well it takes a while to sink in!

Why did the man eat ten tins of baked beans?
He wanted to go wind surfing!

What do you get if you cross a birthday cake and a can of baked beans?
A cake that blows out its own candles!

What's brown and smelly and sits on a piano stool?
Beethoven's last movement!

What smells and shoots at people?
A septic tank!

What's brown and sounds like a bell?
Dung!

it was
the dog!

What do you get if you cross a skunk and an owl?
A bird that stinks but doesn't give a hoot!

What do you get if you cross a skunk and a balloon?
A creature that stinks to high heaven!

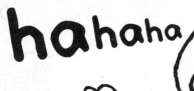

ha ha ha

What do you get if you cross a skunk and a horse?
Whinny The Pooh!

What do you get if you cross a rug and an elephant?
A large pile on the floor!

17

Why do you call your dog Carpenter?
He keeps doing little jobs around the house!

Why do you call your cat Rain?
He keeps leaving puddles everywhere!

What wears a coat all winter and pants all summer?
A dog!

What do you call a flying skunk?
A *smellicopter!*

What do you get if you
walk under a cow?
A *pat on the head!*

Why couldn't cavemen
hear a pterodactyl go
to the toilet?
Because it has a silent 'p'!

hahaha

What do you get if you cross an elephant and a bottle of laxative?
Out of the way!

What did the judge say when the skunk was on trial?
Odour in court!

Did you hear the joke about the skunk?
Never mind, it stinks!

What do you get if you cross a skunk and a boomerang? *A smell that keeps coming back!*

How many skunks do you need to make a house really smelly?
Just a phew!

What do you get if you cross a skunk and a dinosaur?
A stinkasaurus!

What did the baby skunk want to be
when he grew up?
A big stinker!

What did the forgetful skunk say when
the wind changed direction?
*It's all coming back
to me now!*

hahaha

What does a bumble bee sit on?
His beehind!

Why did the bumble
bee fly with his legs crossed?
He was heading for a BP station!

 hahah**a**

What do you get if you
cross a canary and a
seagull?
*A bird that makes a mess
on your head and then
apologises!*

Two pigeons are bored.

"I know what we
can do," says one of them.

"Let's go over to that car showroom and
I'll put down a deposit on a new car!"

Why did the skunk buy
four boxes of tissues?
Because he had a
stinking cold!

Two skunks were being chased by a bear.
As the bear got closer, one of the skunks
said, "Whatever shall we do?"
"Let us spray!" replied the other.

What do you get if
you cross a chicken
and a skunk?
A fowl smell!

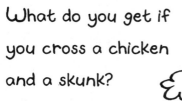

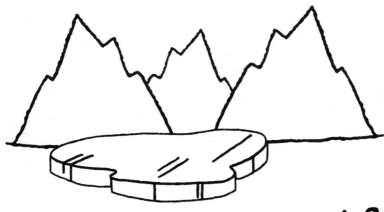

What do polar bears
get from sitting on
ice for too long?
Polaroids!

hahaha

How do you stop a dog from smelling? Cut off his nose!

hahaha

My dog is so lazy! Even when I water the garden he won't even lift a leg to help!

My dog saw a garden fence with a "Wet Paint" sign on it. So he did!

What do you get if you cross an elephant and a budgie?

A very messy cage!

What smells most in a zoo?

Your nose!

What do you get if you cross a chicken with a cement mixer?
A brick layer!

Why was the stable hand unhappy?
His work kept piling up!

How do you make mice smell nice?
You use a mousewash!

How do you turn ants into underwear?
Put a 'P' in front of them!

A man returned his new puppy to the pet shop.

"You said this dog was house trained!" he moaned, "But he goes to the toilet all over the house!"

"He is house trained", replied the shopkeeper "He won't go anywhere else!"

parp

medical mayhem

Patient: Doctor, Doctor, I keep breaking wind. Is there anything you can suggest?

Doctor: Yes, take up wind surfing!

Patient: Doctor, Doctor, my husband's wind smells like rotting fish!

Doctor: The poor sole!

Patient: Doctor, Doctor, I'm
   going bald, is there any cure?

Doctor: Yes, put a kilo of manure
   on your head every morning.

Patient: And that will stop my
   hair falling out?

Doctor: No, but nobody will come
near enough to you to notice
you're bald!

Patient: Doctor, Doctor, I'd like
   something to take this awful
   smell away.

Doctor: So would I!

Patient: Doctor, Doctor, I tend to flush a lot.

Doctor: Don't worry, it's just a normal chain reaction!

Patient: Doctor, Doctor, I keep thinking I'm a toilet!

Doctor: I thought you were looking rather flushed!

Patient: Doctor, Doctor, can you give me something for wind?

Doctor: Here, take this kite!

Patient: Doctor, Doctor, there is something wrong with my tummy!

Doctor: Well keep your jumper on and nobody will notice!

Who exploded at the Battle of
Waterloo?
Napoleon Blownapart!

What has a bottom at its top?
A leg!

ha**ha**ha

family misfortunes

There is an awful smell coming from downstairs near your Aunt Flo.

Cellar?

Do you think we could get a good price!

A wife was fed up with her husband's wind problem.

"You should be a weatherman," she said.

"Why?" her husband replied.

"Because you are such an expert on wind!"

Brother: Why does mum make dad sleep under the bed?

Sister: Because he drives her potty!

What's the worst thing you can do to your sister while she's wearing baggy underwear?
Nick'er elastic!

ha haha

The boy down the street said you smelt so much you weren't fit to live with pigs. What did you say?
I stood up for you, I said of course you were fit to live with pigs!

parp

Son, you smell like a pig! You know what a pig is?
Yes, Dad, the son of a hog!

Girl: Do you know anyone who has been on the TV?

Boy: My little brother did once, but he uses the toilet now!

Boy: Why was your dad thrown out of the council meeting?

Girl: He passed the wrong sort of motion!

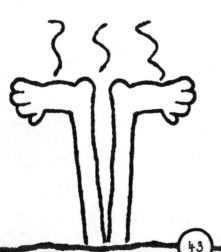

My brother is built upside down. His nose runs and his feet smell!

What does your husband do for a living?

He's a pig farmer.

I thought that he had a certain air about him!

Husband: Will you still love me when I'm old, smelly and ugly?

Wife: Of course I do!

parp

Mother: Do you realise that we have been in Paris for the whole weekend and haven't visited the Louvre yet?

Father: I do, I expect it's the different food we're eating here!

hahaha

Mum: What a filthy mess you look!

Girl: Sorry, Mum, I slipped and fell in a cow pat.

mum: What, in your brand new jacket?

Girl: Well I didn't get time to change!

An old saying –
Man who drop watch
in toilet – in for a
smelly time!

My bother has such a wind problem!
Really?
*Yes. The police arrested him for air
pollution!*

What do you get if
you eat baked beans
and onions?
Tear gas!

knock

knock

Knock Knock
Who's there?
Abbey!
Abbey who?

Abbey stung me on the bum!

Knock Knock
Who's there?
Adjust!
Adjust who?

Adjust made a mess on the floor!

Knock Knock
Who's there?
Ali!
Ali who?

Ali-luyah, at last the toilets free!

Knock Knock
Who's there?
Alec!
Alec who?

Alec to pick my nose!

Knock Knock
Who's there?
Andrew!
Andrew who?

Andrew on the
toilet wall!

Knock Knock
Who's there?
Armageddon!
Armageddon who?

Armageddon
getting out of
here, it stinks!

Knock Knock
Who's there?
Bea!
Bea who?

Bea sweet
and wipe
the seat!

Knock Knock
Who's there?
Annie!
Annie who?

Annie one seen
the toilet rolls,
we've run out!

Knock Knock
Who's there?
Canoe!
Canoe who?

Canoe flush the
loo please!

Knock Knock
Who's there?
Blue!
Blue who?

Blue your nose
and stop
sniffing!

Knock Knock
Who's there?
Butter!
Butter who?

Butter be quick,
I really need
to go!

Knock Knock
Who's there?
Ben!
Ben who?

Ben waiting a
long time for
the toilet!

Knock Knock
Who's there?
Colin!
Colin who?

*Colin the doctor,
I've got the runs!*

Knock Knock
Who's there?
Clare!
Clare who?

*Clare the air
with air
freshener!*

Knock Knock
Who's there?
Deceit!
Deceit who?

Deceit of your
trousers
looks wet!

Knock Knock
Who's there?
Danielle!
Danielle who?

Danielle at me,
it was the dog!

Knock Knock
Who's there?
Fergie!
Fergie who?

Fergie-dness sake let me in I'm bursting!

Knock Knock
Who's there?
Doughnut!
Doughnut who?

Doughnut go in the toilet, it stinks in there!

Knock Knock
Who's there?
Hope!
Hope who?

Hope you'll soon be done!

Knock Knock
Who's there?
Hawaii!
Hawaii who?

Hawaii was fine until I smelt that!

Knock Knock
Who's there?
Muppet!
Muppet who?

Muppet it
up, what a
mess!

Knock Knock
Who's there?
Jam!
Jam who?

Jam mind,
I'd like some
privacy in here!

Knock Knock
Who's there?
Jenny!
Jenny who?

Jenny'd any help
in there?

Knock Knock
Who's there?
Juliet!

Juliet who?

Juliet the same
amount but
she's okay!

Knock Knock
Who's there?
Luxembourg!
Luxembourg who?

Luxembourg just did it on your head!

Knock Knock
Who's there?
Mickey!
Mickey who?

Mickey's stuck in the lock, help I'm stuck in here!

Knock Knock
Who's there?
Phew!
Phew who?

Phew, what a
stink, have you
let one rip?

Knock Knock
Who's there?
Paul!
Paul who?

Paul the chain
when you're
finished!

Knock Knock
Who's there?
Nick!
Nick who?

Nick R Elastic!

Knock Knock
Who's there?
Ooze!
Ooze who?

Ooze made the

seat all wet?

Knock Knock
Who's there?
Sonia!
Sonia who?

Sonia your shoe, wipe your feet before you come in!

Knock Knock
Who's there?
Saul!
Saul who?

Saul over your shoes, it stinks!

Knock Knock
Who's there?
Summertime!
Summertime who?

Summertime you
really do smell!

Knock Knock
Who's there?
Stan!
Stan who?

Stan back I'm
going to let
one rip!

Knock Knock
Who's there?
You!
You who?

You who! Is there anybody in there?

Knock Knock
Who's there?
Statue!
Statue who?

Statue did that?

random
whiffs

What happened to the dog that ate garlic?
His bark was worse than his bite!

When is underwear like flowers?
When the flowers are bloomers!

What do you get if you pull your pants as high as your neck?
A chest of drawers!

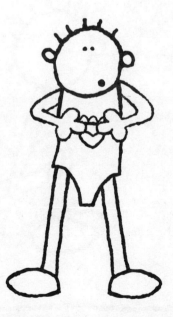

What has two legs, one wheel and stinks?
A wheelbarrow of manure!

What smells, runs all day and lies about at night with it's tongue hanging out?
A pair of old trainers!

What should you do if your nose goes on strike?
Picket!

A skeleton was thinking about breaking wind at a party.
He was too scared to though, he just didn't have the guts!

ha ha ha

What are you going to do with all that manure?
I'm going to put it on my strawberries.
Yuk! I put sugar and cream on mine!

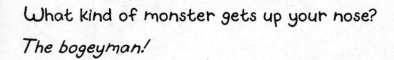

What kind of monster gets up your nose?
The bogeyman!

What happened to the thief who stole a ton of prunes? *He was on the run for weeks!*

What do you call a man who never uses a tissue? *Greensleeves!*

How do poos greet
one another?
How do you do-do!

parp

What's an ig?
An Eskimo house without a loo!

Why is football so messy?

Because all the players dribble!

Hello, you're through to the Incontinence Hotline...

Can you hold, please?

I feel really sick, what shall I do?

You'll soon find out!

What is red and stupid?

A blood clot!

What did the
toothpaste say to
the toothbrush?
*Pinch my bottom and
I'll meet you outside!*

ha haha

What did one eye say to the other?
Between us is something that smells!

If frozen water is iced water,
what is frozen ink?
Iced ink
I know you do, phew!

real
stinkers

Start a new movement, eat a prune!

parp

If you sprinkle when you tinkle, be a sweetie and wipe the seatie!

People using this toilet are requested to remain seated throughout the entire performance!

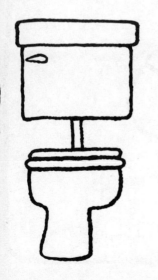
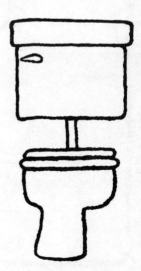

hahaha

We aim to please!
You aim too! Please!

What smells most in a zoo? Your nose!

James Bond rules OOK!

I never used to be able to finish anything, but now I ...

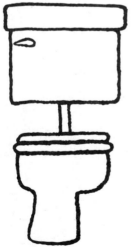

Samson was a strong man,
He could break an iron hoop,
But he never could have done this feat,
If he'd lived on school soup!

Bad spellers of the world, untie!

Here I sit,
What a caper,
I have to poo,
But I'm out of paper!

As you're reading what I've put,
You are weeing on your foot!

Personal
smells rule
BO!

Roses are red,
Violets are blue,
Most poems rhyme,
But this one doesn't!

While you're sitting on the toilet you see written on the stall door:

Congratulations! You've won one free game of Toilet Tennis!

Look Right ... →→→→→ O Look Left ...

Look Right ... O ←←←← O
             →→→

Look Right ... O ←← O Look Left ...

Notice on bottom of toilet door: Beware of limbo dancers!

ha**ha**ha

parp
Incontinence Matters
Phil Mepants
Incurable Wind Problems
I Malone
Lose That Beer Belly
Buster Gutt
Getting rid of Diarrhoea
Watts E Dunn
hahaha

If you're an American when you go into the bathroom, and an American when you come out, what are you when you're in the bathroom?
Eur – o – pean.

If Batman is so smart, why does he wear his pants outside his trousers?

Humpty Dumpty was pushed!

What's a dirty book? *One that's been dropped down a toilet!*

bang on the door™ ©

silly billy

Follow the adventures of Silly Billy —
the silliest boy in the WHOLE world.

TIME OUT

Silly Billy has a brand new watch...
But he doesn't quite know how to use it.
When its alarm goes off one hour early
Silly Billy decides to get HIMSELF
ready for school. And that's when the
trouble starts...

And coming soon...

POOL FOOL

Collins

An imprint of HarperCollins*Publishers*

bang on the door ™ ©

drama queen

Drama Queen makes a drama out of
EVERYTHING. Read about her
latest adventure in...

PUPPY LOVE

Drama Queen knows EXACTLY what
she wants, a sweet, cuddly puppy all of
her very own. But her mum and dad are
not impressed! Then her nanny Leo has
an idea... But will it put Drama Queen
off dogs for ever?

And coming soon...

STAGE STRUCK

Collins

An imprint of HarperCollins*Publishers*

bang on the door™©

friends

Together we make things happen!

Meet Spex, Jude, Tiger,
Sugar, Spice, Flash and Cookie.
Follow their adventures as
they set up a newspaper and
report on crimes, local issues
and Tiger's mum's cooking!

FRIENDS
The Friends set up the *Sunnyvale Standard* to
fifififight the plans of a dastardly property developer.

FRIENDS UNITED
Disaster! The local pool has been closed down –
and just before the summer hols! It's a race
against time as the Friends swing into action
to save their pool.

And coming soon...

FRIENDS AGAIN
The Friends discover local animals are in danger and
tempers are running high. Can they pull together...
and catch the culprit?

An imprint of HarperCollinsPublishers

bang on the door™©

silly billy

Read the next adventure of Silly Billy —
the silliest boy in the WHOLE world.

POOL FOOL

Silly Billy can't wait to get to school
today. It's swimming class this morning,
and he loves to splash around in the pool.
But he's forgotten to bring something
VERY important...
And what IS Silly Billy doing with
those armbands?

((Collins

🕮 *An imprint of* HarperCollins*Publishers*

bang on the door™©

drama queen

Drama Queen makes a drama out of
EVERYTHING. Read about her latest
adventure in . . .

STAGE STRUCK

Drama Queen is very excited!
She loves to dance and sing and act
and she is desperate to be Snow White
in the school play.
But will she get the part?
And who will play Prince Charming?

((Collins

🔲 *An imprint of HarperCollinsPublishers*

bang on the door™©

Collect 5 tokens and get a free poster!*

All you have to do is collect five funky tokens!
You can snip one from any of these cool Bang on the Door books!

0 00 715209 4

0 00 715309 0

0 00 715212 4

0 00 715210 8

Send 5 tokens with a completed coupon to: Bang on the Door Poster Offer

PO Box 142, Horsham, RH13 5FJ (UK residents)

c/- HarperCollins Publishers (NZ) Ltd,
PO Box 1, Auckland (NZ residents)

c/- HarperCollins Publishers, PO Box 321,
Pymble NSW 2073, Australia
(for Australian residents)

0 00 715220 5

- -

First name: .... Surname: ....

Address: ....

....

....

Postcode: .... Child's date of birth: ...... / .... / ....

email address: ....

Signature of parent/guardian: ....

Tick here if you do not wish to receive further information about children's books ☐

PJ1

I token

Terms and Conditions: Proof of sending cannot be considered proof of receipt.
Not redeemable for cash. Please allow 28 days for delivery. Photocopied tokens not accepted.
Offer open to UK, New Zealand and Australia only while stocks last.*rrp £3.99